T0380715

THE
KINGDOM
of GOD

PATRICK ELLISON

WESTBOW
PRESS®
A DIVISION OF THOMAS NELSON
& ZONDERVAN

WestBow Press books may be ordered through booksellers or by contacting:

WestBow Press
A Division of Thomas Nelson & Zondervan
1663 Liberty Drive
Bloomington, IN 47403
www.westbowpress.com
844-714-3454

The Holy Bible, English Standard Version. ESV® Text Edition: 2016. Copyright © 2001 by Crossway Bibles, a publishing ministry of Good News Publishers.

ISBN: 979-8-3850-2796-5 (sc)
ISBN: 979-8-3850-2797-2 (hc)
ISBN: 979-8-3850-2798-9 (e)

Library of Congress Control Number: 2024912585

Print information available on the last page.

WestBow Press rev. date: 07/25/2024

ACKNOWLEDGEMENTS

I wanted to give a special thanks to my beautiful wife Karineh, for encouraging me, and supporting me during the writing and publishing process. I would also like to thank my pastor, Jeremey Smiley, for reviewing this book, and giving wise counsel during the editing process. Last but not least, I am thankful for my family, and the Navigators Young Adults Ministry at Awaken Great Bay Calvary Church, for encouraging me while writing this book.

ACKNOWLEDGMENTS

INTRODUCTION

What is the Kingdom of God?
What are its Characteristics?
What Old Testament scriptures prophesy the coming King?
How does the Kingdom of God operate?
What is the Gospel of the Kingdom?

These are the main questions of this study. It is my goal to argue from the scriptural narrative about the Kingdom of God, and it's relevancy for believers today. Living with an awareness of the Kingdom might in some cases have individual applications, and some universal applications. I touch on some of each in this book, but you as the reader should search out for yourselves what God would have you focus on for furtherance of his will and influence both in your personal life, and in the communities you are apart of. My prayer is that this book will give us some perspective on a subject that by and large is foreign to a lot of western Christians. It is my prayer that this work will be used to cause believers to talk about, think about, teach about, and study the Bible about the Kingdom. I will be quoting scripture from the English Standard Version. May the Lord bless you and give you wisdom from on high.

WHAT IS THE KINGDOM OF GOD?

....

When we read the scriptures, we hear much about the Kingdom of God. From Genesis to the psalms, the law and the prophets, Old Testament to New Testament, the Kingdom of heaven, or even the throne of David/ the Davidic Kingdom is everywhere. But what exactly is it? We pray "your kingdom come" but sometimes as believers, we struggle to grasp what that specifically means, and how to live in light of that. Some of us don't know how it fits into our theology now, so we throw it into sometime in the future, and thus, make it inapplicable for our faith and practice. Let us search the scriptures for wisdom into the nature of the Kingdom.

....

Chapter 1

. . . .

WHAT'S A KINGDOM?

In seeking to understand Gods Kingdom, we first need to understand what a kingdom is in general. Just because we define a word one way, that doesn't necessarily mean God does when communicating something to his people, but nonetheless the scriptures use certain words for a kingdom, so we will stick with the definition of those words.

There are two Hebrew words for kingdom. One is mamlāḵāh, see the definition below. This word has the connotation of royalty, and has been translated as royalty in English. I think this word means royal reign. It seems to imply a country or state.
H4467 מַמְלָכָה

[Analytics]
kingdom (320x) H4467 (117x)

[Kohlenberger/Mounce Hebrew]
gk H4930 | s H4467 מַמְלָכָה mamlāḵāh 117x
n.f. [4887]. kingdom, royal dominion, reign. → dominion; kingdom; kingship.

The other word in Hebrew is mal**k**u**t**, which is a similar idea but different in that this word seems to imply an empire, and is used also as the reign of a king more than mamlā**k**āh seems to be.

kingdom H4438 מַלְכוּת, מַלְכָת, מַלְכַת, מַלְכָיָה

[Analytics]
kingdom (320x) H4438 (90x)

[Kohlenberger/Mounce Hebrew]
gk H4895 | s H4438 מַלְכוּת mal**k**u**t** 91x
n.f. [4889; cf. 4887; 10424]. kingdom, empire, realm; reign, royal power, position as a king. → dominion; kingdom; kingship; power.

In the New Testament, the Greek word for kingdom is basileia, the region or country governed by a king.

kingdom G0932 βασιλεία

[Analytics]
kingdom (320x) G0932 (161x)

[Mounce Greek Dictionary]
gk G993 | s G932 βασιλεία basileia 162x
a kingdom, realm, the region or country governed by a king; kingly power, authority, dominion, reign; royal dignity, the title and honor of king; ἡ βασιλεία, Mt. 9:35, ἡ βασιλεία τοῦ θεοῦ or τοῦ Χριστοῦ or τοῦ οὐρανοῦ or τῶν οὐρανῶν, the reign or kingdom of the Messiah, both in a false and true conception of it; used also with various limitation, of its administration and coming history, as in the parables; its distinctive nature, Rom. 14:17; its requirements, privileges, rewards, consummation → dominion; kingdom; reign; rule.

Putting all of this together, the biblical definition of a kingdom seems to be a place, realm, or empire ruled by a king. Wherever the king has jurisdiction or authority over others that is where his kingdom is. It is the sphere of one's control, where that one rules. So the Kingdom of God is the same in some sense. God's Kingdom is the place where God is King, and where the realm of his authority is.

Chapter 2

. . . .

RULERS RULE

Having defined a kingdom, which is the area in which a king has the authority, jurisdiction, and power to rule, we have another pressing question: what does it mean to rule? How do kings rule? How does our God use his authority?

Matthew 20:25-28 "But Jesus called them to him and said, "You know that the rulers of the Gentiles lord it over them, and their great ones exercise authority over them. 26 It shall not be so among you. But whoever would be great among you must be your servant, 27 and whoever would be first among you must be your slave, 28 even as the Son of Man came not to be served but to serve, and to give his life as a ransom for many."

Here is one difference in how the world rules, and how God rules. The kings of the world use their authority to oppress and bully people. They use their rule to coerce, threaten, and enslave people for their own benefit. But Jesus Christ our King rules with a servants heart, having our best interest in mind. Many kings would ask their subjects to die for them, but our King chose to die for us. In doing so, he demonstrated to us that the heart behind having Kingdom authority is to protect and provide for those you have authority over. Not to indulge yourself and be served.

He leads by serving, and he serves by leading. The purpose of leading is for the growth and upbuilding of those who are being led. Ecclesiastes 5:9,"But this is gain for a land in every way: a king committed to cultivated fields." Solomon didn't just say this about farmlands and crops. In verses preceding this, he is talking about when governmental systems oppress God's people, and poor people. So in the context, he is saying that it is beneficial for people who have a leader dedicated to their growth.

This is great news! Our God, who is our King, uses his authority to serve and give to his subjects. But the question still remains. What does it mean to have authority over something? What does it mean to rule?

Kings, when exercising authority, usually make judgments and decisions about things, and give decrees or commands that his subjects follow. Our Lord does this too. God makes Judgements, decrees, decisions, and commands for his people.

Exodus 19:5-6: "Now therefore, if you will indeed obey my voice and keep my covenant, you shall be my treasured possession among all peoples, for all the earth is mine; 6 and you shall be to me a kingdom of priests and a holy nation.' These are the words that you shall speak to the people of Israel."

Here God says to Israel that if they will submit themselves to Gods covenant that they will be his people and apart of his kingdom. In other words, if they let God rule them, he will be their ruler. Being a Kingdom of priests means that those who walk in covenant with God will be priestly in that they will be representatives for other people in the sight of God. This is a privilege and a responsibility. The nation of Israel in right relationship with God would serve as salt to the surrounding nations, by preserving them from wrath by praying as a priestly people who stand in the gap. Priests also offer up sacrifices, which points to both us offering up the once and for all sacrifice of Jesus for our cleansing of sin, and also what is known as a sacrifice of praise. A sacrifice of praise is a phrase repeated in the Psalms, and is also mentioned in the book of Hebrews. Our prayers and giving of thanks to God are like a good smelling perfume to him. Jesus is the high priest of our confession, because his covenant with the Father, and sacrifice made to the Father, is applied to us. In the New Covenant that was established by King Jesus, we are brought under the rule of the Father through the obedience and blood of the Son. Revelation 1:5-6 "To him who loves us and has freed us from our sins by his blood 6 and made us a kingdom, priests to his God and Father, to him be glory and dominion forever and ever. Amen."

In the New Covenant our King still gives us commandments, shows us royal will, and judges us. We are commanded to love one another with the love that he loves us with. He also tells us that we must die to ourselves, pick up our cross, and follow him. We are commanded to stop sinning, by putting to death the vices that our bodies desire. Our sanctification is his will. Thankfulness at all times is his will, and so is rejoicing in him. We are to pray ceaselessly, praying in the Holy Spirit. There are many other examples of the King's will in the New Testament. God judges us and makes decisions about us now, and one day we will stand before him to give an account for everything. The worthless will be burned up, and the profitable shall remain.

So then, when we pray, "your Kingdom come, your will be done" we are asking that the Father would rule all aspects of our life and of the earth, and that he would tell us what to do. As Christians, we should earnestly desire for Christ to give us his commandments, his will day to day, and his judgments. The church is a priesthood then, offering to the Father the sacrifice of Jesus for ourselves, and interceding for others around us.

Chapter 3

....

A BETTER COUNTRY

Hebrews 11:13-16," These all died in faith, not having received the things promised, but having seen them and greeted them from afar, and having acknowledged that they were strangers and exiles on the earth. 14 For people who speak thus make it clear that they are seeking a homeland. 15 If they had been thinking of that land from which they had gone out, they would have had opportunity to return. 16 But as it is, they desire a better country, that is, a heavenly one. Therefore God is not ashamed to be called their God, for he has prepared for them a city."

Romans 4:13 "For the promise to Abraham and his offspring that he would be heir of the world did not come through the law but through the righteousness of faith"

We are the sons and daughters of Abraham, who is promised the world as his inheritance. These scriptures point to him in his wanderings, faith journey, and trials looking for a land of Heaven on Earth. God had promised him that through his seed, every family on earth would receive blessing. God even changed his name, and promised that he would be the father of many nations. As we know, all of the promises of God are applied to Christ, and come through Christ. Through Jesus, all families in the world are to be blessed with salvation. Salvation is delivering us from the domain of darkness, and transferring us into the Kingdom of the beloved son, Colossians 1:13 paraphrased. The angel told the Virgin Mary in Matthew 1 to name him Jesus, because he would save his people from their sin. Being saved from sin is multi-faceted. We are saved from sins penalty now, which is death and Hell. In this life, we are to become more set apart and grow into transformation. That is the salvation from sins power, and pleasure. And on the last day, death will be thrown into Hell, and we will be fully renewed, along with the universe. This is salvation from sin's presence. In Jesus, Abraham is the father of nations, because Abraham is father to all who become righteous by faith. Jesus is King above all kings, and ruler of all mankind. This is why Jesus said that Abraham rejoiced to see his day in John 8:56. He saw the promise that Jesus would be exalted, and one day give us a land that is from God, coming down from Heaven. When given this land, we enter into it as heirs who steward it.

What is the Kingdom of God? I hope that in these chapters I have given a definition that is persuasive and understandable. In a nutshell, a kingdom is the place where one has jurisdiction and power to do what he wants. God is King over everything and everyone by that definition, he has authority over all creation. The earth is the Lords, and all that is in it. So he is King over all. At the same time, scripture teaches that when Adam, who was Gods steward of creation, fell into sin, he gave over his dominion to Satan. Adam was charged with subduing creation, thus by Gods command being a steward type king over it. Him falling brought the creation under a curse. Satan is called the God of this world. That's why God became a man. Jesus was offered the kingdoms of the world by Satan, without the cross. Jesus refused, but instead paid for the sin of man on the cross, and conquered Satan. He never sinned, so he could both be a sacrifice for us but also be the rightful king of the world as a man. He could usher in a new Eden. He is the firstborn from the dead, being the first fruit of the new creation. We also are called first fruits, because we are in Christ. Jesus is the second Adam who puts many under righteousness, as a new head of the covenant and as Gods king over creation, who promises to make all things new. He is both sovereign over all created things, and he wants his image bearers to reign with him. We are called the co-heirs with Christ. By his merit, we will enter and inherit the true promise land.

KINGDOM CHARACTERISTICS

....

The Kingdom of God is not an abstract thing. There are characteristics that define what it is accurately, and there are things that are opposed to the kingdom, which of course show opposite characteristics than the Kingdom. What does the Bible teach us about what the Kingdom is like?

....

Chapter 4

....

WHERE IS HEAVEN?

When most western believers think of Heavens Kingdom, we imagine it to just be a place we go after we die. It is a blissful paradise in the sky that the faithful go to forever as our soul leaves our body and floats away. We need to unlearn that, it isn't biblical. It is true that when a Christian dies, they go to heaven to be with Christ. However, the nature of the Kingdom is more nuanced than that.

Luke 17:20-21 "Being asked by the Pharisees when the kingdom of God would come, he answered them, "The kingdom of God is not coming in ways that can be observed, 21 nor will they say, 'Look, here it is!' or 'There!' for behold, the kingdom of God is in the midst of you."

The Kingdom is with us, and in us as his disciples. Heaven is an authority that is above us, that rules over us. Every time we submit something for God to use and control, we are putting that thing into the Kingdom of God. Whatever is in the Kingdom, is in Heaven. When Christ returns, he will make a new Heaven and a new Earth. This is where we get glorified bodies like his. This is when his Kingdom will rule all things, physical and spiritual. Right now, we do go into Christ's presence when we die, but not in fullness. Our spirit and soul will be with him, but not our physical bodies. This happens during the resurrection. This is why Jesus said that it isn't coming in ways you can observe: As of now, the Kingdom is spiritual, as opposed to spiritual and physical in nature. Spiritual doesn't mean fake, it just means immaterial. The rule of God has physical implications even now, and comes to Earth now, but the Kingdom has not come in fullness yet, because not all things are made new under the lordship of Jesus. Heaven is not only a place we go to, but a place that comes to us. Jesus taught in the sermon on the mount not to swear by Heaven, because it is Gods throne. The throne is the place that someone rules from. This is why Heaven is associated with the sky, because the skies are above us. Just as the skies are above us, so God's rule, and where he rules from, is over us. Yes, the Bible talks a lot about our treasures and our house, that is, our new bodies, being stored up in the Heavens for us. The last chapter of the Bible describes a heavenly Jerusalem coming down to Earth, so our ultimate destination as Christians is not a disembodied existence in a spiritual realm called Heaven. But rather, our ultimate destination is with new glorified bodies on Earth, but a new one that has been made one with Heaven. Jesus spoke much more about Heaven coming to us than he did about us going to Heaven when we die. What makes Heaven so great is who is in charge there. If Christ is in you, ruling you, then you are a place where Heaven and Earth meet. Our spirit is already sitting with Christ in Heaven, because our spirit is now alive to our master.

Chapter 5

. . . .

NOT OF THIS WORLD, BUT OVER IT

The title of this chapter is one way to describe the Kingdom in its relation to authority on Earth currently.

John 8:36 "Jesus answered, "My kingdom is not of this world. If my kingdom were of this world, my servants would have been fighting, that I might not be delivered over to the Jews. But my kingdom is not from the world."

Jesus says his kingdom is not of this world. He rules in not a worldly, but a heavenly Kingdom. Jesus is King, but he is not physically on Earth ruling from an office or government building. But in Daniel it says,

"...till you know that the Most High rules the kingdom of men and gives it to whom he will." Daniel 4:25.

So Jesus says that his Kingdom is not a worldly Kingdom, but Daniel says that God does rule the kingdoms of man. How do we reconcile these two truths? The Kingdom of God is not a worldly Kingdom in that its value system is not man's. And also, he isn't ruling from Earth, but from Heaven. But God does rule over people, even when they don't know it. He appointed every ruler, and worked all of his purposes through them, even though they were against God in many cases, and had a completely different value system to say the least. Then why pray for rulers? Why pray that they would do God's will, if God is going to accomplish his will anyways? Some have said the purpose is to change us. I don't buy it. It's true that prayer changes us, but this isn't the only reason we are supposed to pray for rulers. We are told in scripture to pray for them so that we will live in peace and security. If you are a parent, then God appointed you to be the parent of your child. Do you need prayer to be a good father or mother? Even though God will accomplish his purposes for you and your child? Of course you need prayer! God calls us to participate in doing his will and extending his Kingdom, even though he is fully capable of working solo. So then, Gods Kingdom is not worldly in its values, but it rules in and above the peoples of Earth. God has always been King, but there was a time when Jesus was not ruling as a human. That's the difference. Jesus rules the nations from heaven now as someone who is fully God, and fully human. He is in Heaven, an immaterial place, with a new material body. He is the first fruit of what will happen to us. He is the sign to everyone that there is a Day of Judgement, and that his people will have new bodies like his, not subjected to any of the effects of sin.

Chapter 6

....

ETERNAL REIGN

All empires in history have a start and end date. The best of kingdoms have crumbled overnight. One comes, another goes. The Kingdom of God is eternal. He will rule forever and ever.

Psalm 145:13   Your kingdom is an everlasting kingdom, and your dominion endures throughout all generations. [The LORD is faithful in all his words and kind in all his works.]

His rule is eternal. He will rule, and us with him, forever and ever. We were created originally to subdue the Earth and rule over it forever the way that God had intended. But it's also a reign of peace for his people. He rules a permanent Kingdom, with a permanent peace.

Isaiah 9:7 "Of the increase of his government and of peace there will be no end, on the throne of David and over his kingdom, to establish it and to uphold it with justice and with righteousness from this time forth and forevermore. The zeal of the LORD of hosts will do this."

Revelation 11:15 Then the seventh angel blew his trumpet, and there were loud voices in heaven, saying, "The kingdom of the world has become the kingdom of our Lord and of his Christ, and he shall reign forever and ever."

There is coming a time when Christ will not just rule the world despite the world. But the kingdoms of the world will be totally consumed by the reign of heaven. Everything will be renewed. Those who were serving the kingdom of Christ, even in seed form, will rule in the world with Christ, because he will give us of his authority.

Chapter 7
. . . .

DELEGATING AUTHORITY

As we have learned, Christ is giving the church authority in the life to come:

Matthew 19:28-30 "Truly, I say to you, in the new world, when the Son of Man will sit on his glorious throne, you who have followed me will also sit on twelve thrones, judging the twelve tribes of Israel. 29 And everyone who has left houses or brothers or sisters or father or mother or children or lands, for my name's sake, will receive a hundredfold and will inherit eternal life. 30 But many who are first will be last, and the last first."

For more on this, read Revelation 2:26 and onward. There are other scriptures that teach that Christ has given us some of his authority now:

Matthew 16:19 "I will give you the keys of the kingdom of heaven, and whatever you bind on earth shall be bound in heaven, and whatever you loose on earth shall be loosed in heaven."

The binding and loosing were legal terms. Being bound means there were restrictions, or things you can't do. And being loosed means that something is permissible. I'm no Greek scholar, but I have learned that another way to translate this is: whatever you bind on Earth will already be bound in Heaven, whatever you loose on Earth will already be loosed in Heaven. So, when the apostles declared something permissible or not, or proclaimed Gods will, they were walking in Christs name and authority. This means the authority the church walks in will not be an authority within itself. It will act in the authority of another. Here is another passage that teaches us about our authority as the church.

Matthew 28:18-20 "And Jesus came and said to them, "All authority in heaven and on earth has been given to me. 19 Go therefore and make disciples of all nations, baptizing them in the name of the Father and of the Son and of the Holy Spirit, 20 teaching them to observe all that I have commanded you. And behold, I am with you always, to the end of the age."

We are commissioned to make disciples of all nations. This is because all authority not only in Heaven, but on Earth belongs to Christ. So when the church makes disciples, baptizes them, and teaches them to do everything that Jesus told us to do, we are walking under the lordship and authority of Christ himself. The only reason we have the right and power to go into territory that was under the control of Satan is because Jesus has already been crowned King of the World.

Luke 10:17-20, "The seventy-two returned with joy, saying, "Lord, even the demons are subject to us in your name!" 18 And he said to them, "I saw Satan fall like lightning from heaven. 19 Behold, I have given you authority to tread on serpents and scorpions, and over all the power of the enemy, and nothing shall hurt you. 20 Nevertheless, do not rejoice in this, that the spirits are subject to you, but rejoice that your names are written in heaven."

We have by the power and authority of the Lord Jesus the authority to cast out demons, and do other signs based in the will of God, for the glory of his name, and to demonstrate his lordship over all. Many in America and western countries don't think this is for today, despite the Bible nowhere teaching that. Jesus sent out not only the 12 apostles, but also 70 disciples in his name and gave authority to heal, cast out demons, cleanse lepers, and raise the dead. They were given this authority before Jesus ascended to Heaven and the Holy Spirit was poured out. In other words, they were not yet born again. And if Jesus gave them this authority who were not born again, and they walked away from Christ in some cases, then why would we think that he wouldn't give the members of his body, who are born again, authority to do such things? We aren't to rejoice in this authority that we are given, but we are to rejoice that our names are in the Book of Life. But that doesn't suggest that in Christ we do not have this authority. The one true God that lives in you has gifted you this as apart of your inheritance. Jesus has given us the authority to tread over the power of our demonic adversaries.

Matthew 18:15-17 "If your brother sins against you, go and tell him his fault, between you and him alone. If he listens to you, you have gained your brother. 16 But if he does not listen, take one or two others along with you, that every charge may be established by the evidence of two or three witnesses. 17 If he refuses to listen to them, tell it to the church. And if he refuses to listen even to the church, let him be to you as a Gentile and a tax collector."

Another authority the church is given now is the authority of church discipline, and the authority of excommunication. When a believer is walking in unrepentant, or unrecognized sin, they are subject to being put out of the assembly, that they may recognize their fault, and repent. We see that excommunication and church discipline are not always the same thing, rather, the final step in church discipline is excommunication. It starts private, and works its way up higher if the person who sinned remains unrepentant. Paul said in his letter that God judges those outside of the church, and church leadership judges those in the church. We couldn't make decisions about other people without Christ giving us the authority to do so.

1 Corinthians 5:3-5 "For though absent in body, I am present in spirit; and as if present, I have already pronounced judgment on the one who did such a thing. 4 When you are assembled in the name of the Lord Jesus and my spirit is present, with the power of our Lord Jesus, 5 you are to deliver this man to Satan for the destruction of the flesh, so that his spirit may be saved in the day of the Lord."

Yes, there have been, and are, abuses when it comes to church discipline. But if done right, it is a painful, but loving gift to help people in their walk with the Lord. It is something that God has given the church the authority to do.

The church has the authority now to judge among ourselves, the authority to disciple all nations, to baptize, to preach and teach, to walk in the gifts of the Holy Spirit, to bind and loose according to the will of God, and to enact church discipline or even excommunication on the unrepentant. Christ is King of a Kingdom now, and therefore has the right to delegate his royal authority.

Chapter 8

．．．．．．．．．．．．．．．．．．．．．．．．．．．．．．．．．

WORD AND POWER

Another thing we need to consider is the precedence of actions vs speaking in God's valuation.

1 Corinthians 4:20, "For the kingdom of God does not consist in talk but in power."

Here we may need some context. In this epistle, Paul is saying that the Corinthians need fathers in Christ, and that's why he had previously sent Timothy to them. In order to have them imitate Paul in his faith and practice. Apparently, it didn't work out so well, because Paul had to come to them and disciple them personally. Some prideful people within the church were acting like Paul would be a no show, and therefore he could never come rebuke them for their errors. So Paul said that when he does come, he won't be looking at what these people said, but what power they were walking in. In the Kingdom, what counts is not what you say or claim, but what you do by the Spirit. You can claim all the dogmas and creeds and confessions of the faith, and be very knowledgeable. However, if you are not walking by the power of the Spirit, then the one who has less to say, or who has less understanding, but is walking by God's power in love is running better than you. You can say that you love God, but if you hate your family in Christ, or are leading a double life, then what you say doesn't matter. Living a life before God fueled by faith through love is the manifestation of the kingdom, and not just one's theology about it, or merely claiming to live for God. We shouldn't be hearers, or speakers of the word, but not doers. Let us not be like the Pharisees who say, and do not do. Yes, we have to have good theology and sound doctrine. But Paul wasn't going to rebuke the arrogant for what they were saying, he was rebuking them for what they were saying not being capable to produce an intended effect. The humble, on the other hand, walk by the power of God, and what they say has the ability to produce by God's power.

On that note, in our study we should also consider how much power is at our Father's disposal, and how that affects us as his children.

1 Chronicles 29:11 Yours, O LORD, is the greatness and the power and the glory and the victory and the majesty, for all that is in the heavens and in the earth is yours. Yours is the kingdom, O LORD, and you are exalted as head above all.

God wins every battle he fights. This makes him mighty to defend his citizens. It is true that we wrestle with principalities and powers, but this is because the Kingdom is on the offense. We are to take part in having all enemies of Christ put under his feet. This scripture about Jesus is the most quoted Old Testament passage in the New Testament:

Psalm 110:1, "The LORD says to my Lord: "Sit at my right hand, until I make your enemies your footstool.""

Paul, explaining this, says:
1 Corinthians 15:21-28 "For as by a man came death, by a man has come also the resurrection of the dead. 22 For as in Adam all

die, so also in Christ shall all be made alive. 23 But each in his own order: Christ the firstfruits, then at his coming those who belong to Christ. 24 Then comes the end, when he delivers the kingdom to God the Father after destroying every rule and every authority and power. 25 For he must reign until he has put all his enemies under his feet. 26 The last enemy to be destroyed is death. 27 For "God has put all things in subjection under his feet." But when it says, "all things are put in subjection," it is plain that he is excepted who put all things in subjection under him. 28 When all things are subjected to him, then the Son himself will also be subjected to him who put all things in subjection under him, that God may be all in all."

No matter what, you will be put under his feet. In the end, every knee will bow, and everyone will acknowledge that Jesus is Lord. Even those who hate him. We have the opportunity now to acknowledge who he is, and to receive mercy. As his soldiers, we are to fight our sin, and the powers of darkness. We do this so Christ will be exalted more and more, and so that unbelievers (who are his enemies by nature and works they do) will be conquered by his love, and made alive in his Kingdom, having their old self be killed with Christ. Either people are conquered by his love, and receive a new nature, or we are conquered by his wrath on the Last Day. We as Christs body are to be apart of his subjecting all rule to him. This speaks of both our individual lives and discipling the nations. As we extend the Kingdom, it is the Father working in us to put everything under Jesus. The Psalms repeatedly refer to God as our fortress and strength. If his Kingdom is powerful enough to be on the offensive, then the King must be powerful enough to be our defense against the flesh, the Devil, and the World. Of course, we have to deny ourselves. We have to fast. We have to pray. We need to stay in the word of God. We need to flee sin. We must gouge out eyes, and cut off hands. But the Holy Spirit who dwells within us is the one who enables us to do all of these things. We can run to him in trials and temptations, because he is there with us to help in times of trouble.

Throughout this book, there is a lot of words like "conquering" "fighting" "putting to death" because the scriptures use that language a lot. However, it is worth mentioning that this is not a call for rebellion against governments, or a call to violence towards people. I think that if you read this in context that you won't think that's what I'm saying, but I need to spell that out. We can't partake in the same sins that has led people to oppress others in order to break free of oppression. Darkness is overcome by light, not more darkness. Jesus didn't conquer the World by the bloodshed of others, but by laying down his own life. He taught us that whoever tries saving his life will lose it, and whoever loses it for his sake finds it. Christianity spreads well by the sword, just not the sword the church is wielding. It is the sword that is against us that causes flourishing. In areas where Christians are heavily persecuted, there is revival. I recently watched the movie :The Hunger Games: The Ballard of Songbirds and Snakes. It was the origin movie for President Snow, who in the hunger games is a brutal dictator. In this movie, the conclusion that Snow comes to is that the world is an arena like the hunger games, and the way forward is by putting down, manipulating, and killing others for self-advancement and preservation. This mindset is a problem for everyone who is not in the kingdom. It causes us to not walk truly in the ways of God, who is the God of the living, but live under the influence of Satan, who held people in his grasp by fear of death. This is why many believers in the west hate Darwinian Theory, which in essence is "the survival of the fittest". That worldview is at odds with Christ, who commands us to be servants of everyone, and not to use our advantages over others for self in any way. In a dog eat dog world, we are to give up ourselves to others, because even if we are devoured, in the end God will give us justice. I am not a pacifist, but I believe that we as the church should follow Christ by giving up our lives and never seek to repay evil with more evil. We conquer by the blood of the lamb, the word of our testimony, and we love not our own lives even unto death, Revelation 12:11 paraphrased.

Of those who are born again, the weakest is greater than the best of people under the Old Covenant:

Matthew 11:11 "Truly, I say to you, among those born of women there has arisen no one greater than John the Baptist. Yet the one who is least in the kingdom of heaven is greater than he."

We are greater because we are now a part of the Kingdom. We are born again into the family of God, and are heirs of the life to come. We put on the new man, who is reborn into the image of God. We are children of the King, so the least is greater than even John the Baptist. As we have seen, God gives his citizens authority, power, and gifts. He expects us to walk in those in fervor and faithfulness. This is very encouraging to us if we want to become more like Jesus, but it's also very convicting, because it means that God has given us everything we need to become holy, and therefore we have no reason or excuse when we walk contrary to the standards he set for us in Christ.

Chapter 9

INCORRUPTIBLE

Human empires can be corrupted, conquered and disintegrate from within. It is not so of Christ's Kingdom.

Hebrews 12:28-29 "Therefore let us be grateful for receiving a kingdom that cannot be shaken, and thus let us offer to God acceptable worship, with reverence and awe, 29 for our God is a consuming fire."

The reason why the Kingdom is unshakable is because of who is ruling it. The Holy and righteous God has the authority. He will reign justly and with righteousness forever.

Hebrews 1:8 But of the Son he says,
"Your throne, O God, is forever and ever, the scepter of uprightness is the scepter of your kingdom."

Any kingdom is built upon the character of its king. If you have a ruler that is quick tempered or violent like a tyrant, then the policies he enacts will be brutal. He will oppress his subjects. If he is charitable, he will build a more generous culture, which has resources for those who are poor, and less fortunate than himself. If he is industrious, you can bet infrastructure will be a part of his rule. Some people say things like, "God won't judge me for my actions, he knows my heart." When I hear that, my response is, "your heart is the reason your hand sins. Somebody can outwardly do the right thing, but inwardly they are full of evil. It may not be pronounced, but their evil will spill out of them, and become apparent. Your heart is corrupt. Repeatedly in the scriptures God asks men this: when will you stop following the dictates of your evil heart?" So just as you can't separate your heart from your hand, so you can't separate a king from his kingdom. That being established, when you learn things about the kingdom of God, just like the law of God, it reveals the character and nature of God. For example, when scripture says, "righteousness and justice are the foundation of his throne" Psalm 97:2, we can learn from Gods throne, which is where he rules from, what God is like. He loves justice and righteousness, it's the foundation of his rules and decrees. This is why our study of the kingdom is so important. Because it teaches us about the character of the Most High. The avenue God expresses his love and traits is by the way that he leads. God expresses his holy character by his standard of holiness to enter into his presence. He is almighty and pure, therefore, his Kingdom will never be corrupted or overthrown.

Chapter 10

....

GREATEST LAW

Mark 12:28-34 "And one of the scribes came up and heard them disputing with one another, and seeing that he answered them well, asked him, "Which commandment is the most important of all?" 29 Jesus answered, "The most important is, 'Hear, O Israel: The Lord our God, the Lord is one. 30 And you shall love the Lord your God with all your heart and with all your soul and with all your mind and with all your strength.' 31 The second is this: 'You shall love your neighbor as yourself.' There is no other commandment greater than these." 32 And the scribe said to him, "You are right, Teacher. You have truly said that he is one, and there is no other besides him. 33 And to love him with all the heart and with all the understanding and with all the strength, and to love one's neighbor as oneself, is much more than all whole burnt offerings and sacrifices." 34 And when Jesus saw that he answered wisely, he said to him, "You are not far from the kingdom of God."

This passage sheds light on an aspect of the Kingdom. What we learn is that it has hierarchical values. It shows us what heavenly emphasis's are. Namely, they are the nature of the King, and love supremely for him, as well as loving as you love yourself. In the new covenant, the standard is actually higher. It isn't to love one another like we love ourselves. But rather, it is to love one another as Jesus loves us. These are the most important things for people of the Kingdom to do in all private devotions and public interactions. If the summary of the law of Moses is to love, then we are commanded to love. If you think deeply about it, you'll realize that's what makes sin as evil as it truly is. Sinning is breaking God's law that he commanded us to do. Since the essence of the law is to love, we sin against love, not an arbitrary, impersonal set of guidelines and restrictions. We have not truly loved as God loves, that is why we need a savior. We can not keep the law, and be justified by the law. Another way to say it is: we can not love the way we are commanded, and we can't be righteous in his sight by our attempts to love, because even if we do the right things, love is usually not our motivation. The scribe realizes the truth about the commandments being about love, and agrees with Jesus on what takes priority. Then Jesus's answer is: you aren't far from the Kingdom. If he would have come in humble faith to the feet of the Lord Jesus, he would have made it into the Kingdom. Our God is the God of love, and so his entire Kingdom, with all of its commandments and benefits, are built on his character of love. It isn't only the highest value, but all of the other values are made because of love. Therefore, everything is subject to love.

Chapter 11

PRIORITIES, PREFERENCES, AND CONVICTIONS

Romans 14:17 "For the kingdom of God is not a matter of eating and drinking but of righteousness and peace and joy in the Holy Spirit."

This is another important aspect of the kingdom. That is, it places more value on righteousness, peace, and joy than it does on the personal convictions of Christians. What can we learn from this in our modern context?

Suppose you have two Christians. One thinks that tattoos are sinful, and that the prohibition in Leviticus is for gentile Christians. Then you have another, who has a full sleeve of ink. What is more important to the Holy Spirit is not the one saying the other is in sin, or the other saying the one is a legalist. What is better is to let both think that they are correct, to the glory of God, and to have the Holy Spirit give you righteousness, peace, and joy by his indwelling. Thus, we learn that our Lord gives us a lot of diversity and freedom in regards to both preferences and convictions. Yes, we have unity, but each citizen in the Kingdom is encouraged to live as they are called, and be who they are in

Christ. When Adam was in the garden, he had the freedom to eat from any tree he wished, except one. He had many options. Our King is not a micro manager, or a dictator. In North Korea, Kim Jon Un made it so the males can have one of five haircuts. The reason being is so the citizens have no freedom, even in how they look. Christ is so much better. He did buy all of us, he owns us completely. Yet he gives us our individuality, and even celebrates it. With that being said, we are not to flaunt this freedom in such a way that discourages other peoples walk. For freedom we have been set free, but not for self-indulgence or belittling. Instead, use it to love and serve others. Paul says "why would you destroy your brother, for whom Christ died, over food?" Romans 14:15 paraphrased. What would it look like if we used our freedom for the benefit of others? Imagine two people completely disagreeing with each other about a personal conviction, yet still having unity. Lots of churches in America would rather divide over carpet color, what style of songs to sing in worship, and plenty of other issues that are neither primary or secondary. The church should always stand for truth, never compromising. But whether or not someone feels comfortable watching Harry Potter for instance, is not an issue worth dividing over. I have a tattoo, and so being at peace for me means that if my tattoo offends someone else, I'll wear a long sleeve shirt around them. Serving in love for them looks like not calling me a foolish vain heathen, even if they think tattoos are sinful. Simply not fighting with each other is a great start, but it isn't enough. Not arguing with someone you don't like isn't synonymous with living at peace with them. Who is easier not to fight with: your neighbor who lives down the street that you don't know too well, or your mother in law? For the record, I have a great relationship with my in-laws. This is an illustration. You have to have the ability to not live at peace with people in order to choose peace. The church should be involved with the lives of others, and oftentimes we don't get along with others in the church. What we usually do is form our own little cliques, and not associate with people who have different convictions than we do. Living at peace with them is choosing to love and be around other people you don't agree with. And doing what you can to not offend them or judge them. The Kingdom priority is being right with God, having his joy in our hearts, and living at peace with one another.

ANTICIPATION AND EXPECTATION

....

John 6:14-15 "When the people saw the sign that he had done, they said, "This is indeed the Prophet who is to come into the world!"15Perceiving then that they were about to come and take him by force to make him king, Jesus withdrew again to the mountain by himself."

In the time of Jesus, many people were eagerly awaiting the promised messiah. That's why in this passage in the gospel of John, they intended to forcibly make him King. The Jews had been suffering for quite some time under the Roman Empire, and they were desperate for the promised branch of David to come, and to destroy the Romans, and make Israel the ruler of the nations. They held on to Old Testament passages that spoke of the Christ who was coming into the World. But what were some of these scriptures?

....

Chapter 12

LION OF JUDAH

Genesis 49:9-10 "Judah is a lion's cub; from the prey, my son, you have gone up. He stooped down; he crouched as a lion and as a lioness; who dares rouse him?10 The scepter shall not depart from Judah, nor the ruler's staff from between his feet, until tribute comes to him; and to him shall be the obedience of the peoples."

This is the first Old Testament passage that describes the messiah as a kingly figure. Jacob was the one who prophesied this, and so it was very early in Jewish history. This was first fulfilled in David, who was of the tribe of Judah, and then ultimately fulfilled in Christ. Jacob prophesied that someone of Judah would rule Israel, he would receive tribute (see Psalm 72:10), and that the people of Israel would obey him. It is true that most of the people of Israel have rejected him, but there is coming a time when there will be a huge revival among the Jewish people. There has been a remnant of Jews who believe from Jesus's time on earth until now, and there will be a time when they will receive him as their rightful King.

Romans 11:11-12 "So I ask, did they stumble in order that they might fall? By no means! Rather, through their trespass salvation has come to the Gentiles, so as to make Israel jealous. 12 Now if their trespass means riches for the world, and if their failure means riches for the Gentiles, how much more will their full inclusion mean!"

Numbers 24:2-9 "And Balaam lifted up his eyes and saw Israel camping tribe by tribe. And the Spirit of God came upon him, 3 and he took up his discourse and said, "The oracle of Balaam the son of Beor, the oracle of the man whose eye is opened, 4 the oracle of him who hears the words of God, who sees the vision of the Almighty, falling down with his eyes uncovered:5 How lovely are your tents, O Jacob, your encampments, O Israel! 6 Like palm groves that stretch afar, like gardens beside a river, like aloes that the LORD has planted, like cedar trees beside the waters. 7 Water shall flow from his buckets, and his seed shall be in many waters; his king shall be higher than Agag, and his kingdom shall be exalted.

8 God brings him out of Egypt and is for him like the horns of the wild ox; he shall eat up the nations, his adversaries, and shall break their bones in pieces and pierce them through with his arrows. 9 He crouched, he lay down like a lion and like a lioness; who will rouse him up? Blessed are those who bless you, and cursed are those who curse you."

Numbers 24:15-17 "And he took up his discourse and said, "The oracle of Balaam the son of Beor, the oracle of the man whose eye is opened, 16 the oracle of him who hears the words of God, and knows the knowledge of the Most High, who sees the vision of the Almighty, falling down with his eyes uncovered: 17 I see him, but not now; I behold him, but not near: a star shall come out of Jacob, and a scepter shall rise out of Israel;"

Balaam lived during the time of Moses, which was roughly 1,500 years before Jesus came in the flesh. This is a prophet who is not

Jewish, and ended up trying to cause Israel to stumble. But in these oracles, it was prophesied that a King would come out of Israel, and this King would lead Israel to victory in battle, and be exalted. It also said that his seed shall be in many waters, suggesting that he will be a king with influence over all people groups, and not Israel alone. There are some parallels with Balaam and the wise men of the nativity scene, who came to the infant Jesus with worship and gifts. In both accounts, gentiles who practices either astrology or divination see a star, in Balaam's case, the star was coming out of Israel, in the Magi's case, they followed a star to Christ. In both cases, they acknowledged that the star signified a King coming into the world, worthy of both fear and praise. Some think that the wise men were from Mesopotamia, because the Magi were a political group of priests in modern day Iran, which is either in or bordering Mesopotamia. We don't know that for certain, but Balaam was from Mesopotamia. It is also interesting to note, that in the Jewish worldview, the stars serve as delegated rulers for the heavens. In the book of Genesis, we learn that God gave the sun and moon to rule days and nights, and the stars served as symbols and signs. So the association with the star and the king is that the king is not earthly, but heavenly. The star coming out of Israel, and hovering over Christ speaks to both his kingship as well as his divinity.

Chapter 13

. . . .

ASKED AND RECEIVED

1 Samuel 8:5, "…Behold, you are old and your sons do not walk in your ways. Now appoint for us a king to judge us like all the nations."

When Samuel the prophet was old, the people of Israel asked for a king. They wanted to be like all of the people around them. They were given Saul for roughly 40 years. The name Saul in Hebrew means "asked for". He was the king they asked for. In his anger God gave Israel a king like everyone else. God knew their motivation: they did not want Yahweh to rule them. He himself said that he was their King. But God rejected Saul, and instead gave the people David, the man after his own heart. The name David means "beloved". I bring this story up because this was a type of what would happen with the Father sending Jesus, the Son. The people of Israel asked again for a king, this time they wanted the messiah from the line of David, but they were asking for a king so that Israel would be sovereign, and the king would lead them to victory over Rome and all other gentile enemies. Ironically, they wanted a king that acted much like the gentile kings that were oppressing them, which Saul also did.They again did not want God to be their ruler, because they hated the way that God ruled. The World hates the values of Heaven, this is evident by people's disobedience regarding service and love, and disobedience by using authority sinfully, by pushing down the poor for self exaltation. Jesus rebuked the Pharisees in Mark 12:40 for taking widow's houses and praying long prayers to look spiritual. The word Jesus uses is " pretense" which in Greek means to make first. But instead of giving a king like the World, The Father sent his beloved Son, who was the image of the Fathers heart. He is the image of God. Jesus is like David in that he is the beloved King that the people didn't ask for, but was the one after God's own heart. He is the true ruler of the people of God. Most people, when they think of God, they imagine a bigger, more glorious version of themselves. We think that God is just like us. David was different. He longed to be more like God, as opposed to trying to conform God into his image. Just as David and his sons had Israel rebel against them, so Jesus also had his own people rebel against him. His plan was always the cross, but that doesn't mean that his betrayal was not sin on the part of those who had him crucified. Yet despite this, God has exalted him above all other rule or authority. Jesus is the name above every other name.

Chapter 14

THE HOUSE OF DAVID

1 Chronicles 17:10-14 "Moreover, I declare to you that the LORD will build you a house. 11 When your days are fulfilled to walk with your fathers, I will raise up your offspring after you, one of your own sons, and I will establish his kingdom. 12 He shall build a house for me, and I will establish his throne forever. 13 I will be to him a father, and he shall be to me a son. I will not take my steadfast love from him, as I took it from him who was before you, 14 but I will confirm him in my house and in my kingdom forever, and his throne shall be established forever.'"

The same thing is said in 2 Samuel 7:12-14. This was spoken to David after he came into Jerusalem, when he asked to build a temple for the Lord. The Lord said no, that he could not. But that Solomon would build a temple, and that the house of David would have a man on the throne forever. David was never called God's son. God never spoke personally to Solomon with that title. During Jesus's baptism and transfiguration God the Father calls Jesus his beloved Son, and that he was pleased with him. Verse 13 is referring primarily to Christ, and secondly to Solomon. Not the other way around. At the time of the Babylonian captivity, and up until the time of Jesus, the people of either Judah or Israel did not have someone from the lineage of David ruling them. This time period is called the intertestamental period, lasting about 400 years. Then about 40 years after Jesus ascended, Jerusalem was destroyed and the people of Israel was dispersed throughout the World. The genealogical records were destroyed, so nobody from then until now knows who is of David's lineage. So we can't confirm if any other messiah is valid. That means that either Jesus was their messiah, or that God broke his promise to David to have someone from his lineage on the throne.We know that he is faithful to fulfill what he promises every single time. The prophets who came out of the Babylonian captivity prophesied about the messiah coming, both his first and second. They didn't believe that God broke his word to David, because he inspired them to prophesy about the anointed one, and Jesus alone matches the description. He is the only one who is both the Son of David, and the Son of God. Christians did not create Jesus's divinity, the Old Testament defines him as the Son of God. If you think that statement does not mean that he is claiming to be God, then why did the Pharisees in John 5 want to kill Jesus for saying he is the Son of God? Because In saying so, Jesus made himself equal with God. The prophet Amos said that the tent of David would be repaired, and that Gentiles would seek God. This points to David's descendent reclaiming his royal influence, and his covering being over the nations as well. In Hebrew, the word for gentiles is the same as the word for nations. The gentiles seeking God because David's tent is repaired is a complex way of pointing to Jesus being exalted, and God fulfilling his word to David about the Kingdom. He does more than we can even picture him doing.

Chapter 15

PRINCE OF PEACE

Isaiah 11: "There shall come forth a shoot from the stump of Jesse and a branch from his roots shall bear fruit. 2 And the Spirit of the LORD shall rest upon him, the Spirit of wisdom and understanding, the Spirit of counsel and might, the Spirit of knowledge and the fear of the LORD.

3 And his delight shall be in the fear of the LORD. He shall not judge by what his eyes see, or decide disputes by what his ears hear, 4 but with righteousness he shall judge the poor, and decide with equity for the meek of the earth; and he shall strike the earth with the rod of his mouth, and with the breath of his lips he shall kill the wicked. 5 Righteousness shall be the belt of his waist, and faithfulness the belt of his loins. Isaiah. 11:6 The wolf shall dwell with the lamb, and the leopard shall lie down with the young goat, and the calf and the lion and the fattened calf together; and a little child shall lead them. 7 The cow and the bear shall graze; their young shall lie down together; and the lion shall eat straw like the ox. 8 The nursing child shall play over the hole of the cobra, and the weaned child shall put his hand on the adder's den. 9 They shall not hurt or destroy in all my holy mountain; for the earth shall be full of the knowledge of the LORD as the waters cover the sea. Is. 11:10 In that day the root of Jesse, who shall stand

as a signal for the peoples—of him shall the nations inquire, and his resting place shall be glorious. Is. 11:11 In that day the Lord will extend his hand yet a second time to recover the remnant that remains of his people, from Assyria, from Egypt, from Pathros, from Cush, from Elam, from Shinar, from Hamath, and from the coastlands of the sea. Is. 11:12 He will raise a signal for the nations and will assemble the banished of Israel, and gather the dispersed of Judah from the four corners of the earth. 13 The jealousy of Ephraim shall depart, and those who harass Judah shall be cut off; Ephraim shall not be jealous of Judah, and Judah shall not harass Ephraim. 14 But they shall swoop down on the shoulder of the Philistines in the west, and together they shall plunder the people of the east. They shall put out their hand against Edom and Moab, and the Ammonites shall obey them. 15 And the LORD will utterly destroy the tongue of the Sea of Egypt, and will wave his hand over the River with his scorching breath, and strike it into seven channels, and he will lead people across in sandals. 16 And there will be a highway from Assyria for the remnant that remains of his people, as there was for Israel when they came up from the land of Egypt."

Zechariah 9:9-10" Rejoice greatly, O daughter of Zion! Shout aloud, O daughter of Jerusalem! Behold, your king is coming to you; righteous and having salvation is he, humble and mounted on a donkey, on a colt, the foal of a donkey. 10 I will cut off the chariot from Ephraim and the war horse from Jerusalem; and the battle bow shall be cut off, and he shall speak peace to the nations; his rule shall be from sea to sea, and from the River to the ends of the earth."

These two prophecies speak about the King bringing peace. In Isaiah, the passage talks about Christ judging righteously, ruling with faithfulness, removing shame from Israel, and bringing peace. Since Jesus didn't set up a worldly kingdom, with its capitol in Jerusalem, and since there was still turmoil, the Jews rejected him as their King. Jesus did defeat the ultimate enemies of Israel and the gentiles on the cross, namely, sin, death, and the principalities of darkness.

Colossians 2:13-16 "And you, who were dead in your trespasses and the uncircumcision of your flesh, God made alive together with him, having forgiven us all our trespasses, 14 by canceling the record of debt that stood against us with its legal demands. This he set aside, nailing it to the cross. 15 He disarmed the rulers and authorities and put them to open shame, by triumphing over them in him."

Jesus also said to take heart in our tribulations, because he has overcome the world. This doesn't mean just that he remained perfect and the world didn't change him. Nor does it paint a picture like Rocky, who put up a good fight with all his heart but still lost. No, the word overcome here is **nikaō**, which means to conquer, subdue, overcome, and overcome in a legal case. So Jesus is saying, "take heart in your tribulations for my sake, I have conquered the world. " The enemies that Jesus conquered are the real enemies that rule the world. It was sin, death, and demonic entities, especially those who do their will through the empires of the world.

And when he returns, he will judge the living and the dead. And in the new creation, there will be peace forever and ever in the World. And this passage will be ultimately fulfilled. It is partially fulfilled with us, because he is now our prince of peace. His peace he left with us, and it is not as the World gives- John 14:27 paraphrased. But one day, in Christ, there will be World peace. We are commanded to be at peace for this reason. We are to model what the future will look like in the here and now. Just like the children of Israel were to be pictures of what Jesus would do through holidays and commandments in the Torah, which is God's law.

The prophecy in Zechariah had it fulfillment during the Palm Sunday passages in the New Testament. When the people cried out "Hosanna!" This meant save us. It was a political cry. The people were happy to accept Jesus as their King at that time because they thought his goal was to overthrow Rome and regain Israel's sovereignty. But even in the Zechariah passage he is a King of peace, not an insurrectionist.

Chapter 16

LION AND LAMB

There are many other scriptures that speak about the other things Jesus would do. Him as King is certainly not the only thing he is. For the Jews in the first century, and really since the time of the Babylonian captivity, the messiah they wanted was a political one primarily. They suffered under evil polytheistic kingdoms, and so the promises they emphasized were what they interpreted as political promises. Before, during, and after Jesus was on Earth, many rose up claiming messianic titles. Almost all of them were revolutionaries, fighting against political oppression. In Acts chapter 5, Gamaliel, a chief Rabbi, mentions some people who claimed messianic titles, and led revolts. According to Josephus, a first century Jewish historian, Judas the Galilean mentioned in Acts led a protest on the census in 6AD, and his revolt died. In Acts 21, the tribune asks Paul if he is the Egyptian who led a revolt. There was an Egyptian man, claiming to be a prophet, who tried to storm Jerusalem. He was stopped and fled into the wilderness. The zealots were a group of Jewish nationalists who often used violence and assassinations for political purposes. One of Jesus's apostles was a zealot named Simon. They neglected scriptures that spoke of him as the suffering servant, the Lamb of God, and the one who would be cut off for his people's sin. In their context, they remembered the Conquering King, but forgot the Suffering Servant. In our context, we have remembered the Suffering Servant, but have forgotten the Conquering King. We have done this by throwing all of the kingly aspects of Jesus into the second coming or the millennium. Yes, some things that Jesus will do as King is specifically for his second coming, like judging the World. But not every aspect of his kingly position and nature are for his return. The first 3 chapters in the book of Revelation are the things that Jesus told the churches in 7 different regions. He would assess their situations, teachings, and attitudes. He would then make decisions on what the churches were supposed to do, and gave consequences if they refused to obey him. Jesus was judging, giving decrees, and warning about disciplinary measures. Those are the roles that a King takes on behalf of his people. We must remember that he is both at the same time the Lamb of God who takes away the sin of the world, and the Lion of the tribe of Judah, who is Lord of all creation.

KINGDOM IN OPERATION: A JOURNEY THROUGH PARABLES

. . . .

When we read Christ's parables, we often see them in an incorrect context. When we look at them, we often see them as separate issues or subjects. We think they are talking about salvation, sanctification, types of people, or hidden principles primarily. They do touch on all of those and more, however, they are not primarily about these things. The parables usually start with "the Kingdom of Heaven is like" or "the Kingdom of God may be compared to". So from the go, Jesus is saying that the parables are first and foremost about the Kingdom. Either showing an aspect of it, or explaining the way it operates. And the other subjects in the parables are those subjects in relation to it.

. . . .

Chapter 17

....

PARABLE OF THE SOWER

Matthew 13:1-23, "That same day Jesus went out of the house and sat beside the sea. 2 And great crowds gathered about him, so that he got into a boat and sat down. And the whole crowd stood on the beach. 3 And he told them many things in parables, saying: "A sower went out to sow. 4 And as he sowed, some seeds fell along the path, and the birds came and devoured them. 5 Other seeds fell on rocky ground, where they did not have much soil, and immediately they sprang up, since they had no depth of soil, 6 but when the sun rose they were scorched. And since they had no root, they withered away. 7 Other seeds fell among thorns, and the thorns grew up and choked them. 8 Other seeds fell on good soil and produced grain, some a hundredfold, some sixty, some thirty. 9 He who has ears, let him hear."

Matt. 13:10 Then the disciples came and said to him, "Why do you speak to them in parables?" 11 And he answered them, "To you it has been given to know the secrets of the kingdom of heaven, but to them it has not been given. 12 For to the one who has, more will be given, and he will have an abundance, but from the one who has not, even what he has will be taken away. 13 This is why I speak to them in parables, because seeing they do not see, and hearing they do not hear, nor do they understand. 14 Indeed, in their case the prophecy of Isaiah is fulfilled that says: ""You will indeed hear but never understand, and you will indeed see but never perceive." 15 For this people's heart has grown dull, and with their ears they can barely hear, and their eyes they have closed, lest they should see with their eyes and hear with their ears and understand with their heart and turn, and I would heal them.'

Matt. 13:16 But blessed are your eyes, for they see, and your ears, for they hear. 17 For truly, I say to you, many prophets and righteous people longed to see what you see, and did not see it, and to hear what you hear, and did not hear it.

Matt. 13:18 "Hear then the parable of the sower: 19 When anyone hears the word of the kingdom and does not understand it, the evil one comes and snatches away what has been sown in his heart. This is what was sown along the path. 20 As for what was sown on rocky ground, this is the one who hears the word and immediately receives it with joy, 21 yet he has no root in himself, but endures for a while, and when tribulation or persecution arises on account of the word, immediately he falls away. 22 As for what was sown among thorns, this is the one who hears the word, but the cares of the world and the deceitfulness of riches choke the word, and it proves unfruitful. 23 As for what was sown on good soil, this is the one who hears the word and understands it. He indeed bears fruit and yields, in one case a hundredfold, in another sixty, and in another thirty."

This is the first of many parables in Matthew 13. When preached, the Kingdom implications are usually not touched on. I don't believe that this is intentional, rather, I don't think that the modern western church knows what to do with the kingdom. Every culture has ideas and values that are emphasized. Often times the church has a worldview that is basically the same as whatever nation they reside in, just Christianized. For instance, America has been defined as a Christian nation, but there is a separation between church and state. So many American Christians think that because our culture believes that, then so does Jesus. We need to evaluate how we think, and what we think. When we think of the separation between church and state, we often think that means Christians really should stay out of all politics, and there should be no involvement from us. We think that our only goal is to teach people how to go to Heaven, and how to cultivate a personal relationship with Jesus, while the World does whatever it wants, without any accountability from the church. We as a people are also a republic, which is democratic because we pick our representatives and leaders by vote. Our political system is about our personal rights and freedoms, and not relying on an individual or group of people to lead us and make decisions on our behalf. So in that context, it makes sense that we don't really emphasize the Kingdom of God. It's a foreign idea to many of us. But just because it's foreign to us, doesn't mean that it was to Jesus. This parable is primarily about the kingdom. In its context, the word being preached is that Christ is King. It's the word of the Kingdom. When some hear that the kingdom is at hand, they do not understand, so Satan steals the word from their hearts. Some hear, and are overjoyed that Christ is now their master, but due to lack of being rooted in the King, they fall away as soon as their loyalty is tested. Others receive the news, but the cares of the current world system, which is Satan's influence and kingdom, causes unfruitfulness. Jesus also mentions the deceitfulness of riches, which when someone serves money, in a sense they are trying to establish their own kingdom, with influence and authority by their wealth. The ones who are thorns either love Satan's kingdom, or their own kingdom more than Christ's, and thus are unfit for it. Then there are those who hear that Christ is King, and submit to his lordship above all else. They have varying amounts of growth in and for the Kingdom they serve. We as the good soil are to abide in our King, and bear fruit. The fruit is the reign and glory of God becoming larger and larger in our lives, and in the world around us. Jesus taught in the sermon on the mount to let our light shine, so that when people see it, they glorify the Father. This is bearing fruit. Not only the works that we do for him, but the works that he has prepare for us bringing glory to his name. This is what Paul meant in Colossians when he prayed that we would be bearing fruit in our good works.

Chapter 18
. . . .

THE PARABLE OF THE
WEEDS OF THE FIELD

Matt. 13:24 He put another parable before them, saying, "The kingdom of heaven may be compared to a man who sowed good seed in his field, 25 but while his men were sleeping, his enemy came and sowed weeds among the wheat and went away. 26 So when the plants came up and bore grain, then the weeds appeared also. 27 And the servants of the master of the house came and said to him, 'Master, did you not sow good seed in your field? How then does it have weeds?' 28 He said to them, 'An enemy has done this.' So the servants said to him, 'Then do you want us to go and gather them?' 29 But he said, 'No, lest in gathering the weeds you root up the wheat along with them. 30 Let both grow together until the harvest, and at harvest time I will tell the reapers, "Gather the weeds first and bind them in bundles to be burned, but gather the wheat into my barn."

Matt. 13:36 Then he left the crowds and went into the house. And his disciples came to him, saying, "Explain to us the parable of the weeds of the field." 37 He answered, "The one who sows the good seed is the Son of Man. 38 The field is the world, and the good seed is the sons of the kingdom. The weeds are the sons of the evil one, 39 and the enemy who sowed them is the devil. The harvest is the end of the age, and the reapers are angels. 40 Just as the weeds are gathered and burned with fire, so will it be at the end of the age. 41 The Son of Man will send his angels, and they will gather out of his kingdom all causes of sin and all law-breakers, 42 and throw them into the fiery furnace. In that place there will be weeping and gnashing of teeth. 43 Then the righteous will shine like the sun in the kingdom of their Father. He who has ears, let him hear."

In this parable, Jesus is preaching the coming Kingdom, and its relation to the Day of Judgment. Again, Christ is preaching that he is the prophesied King from the linage of David. Christs body the church preaches the word on the earth, which is sowing seeds. Also, we are the seeds sown in the world. The wheat is the citizens of heaven. During this process, Satan will be sowing bad seeds, which are his converts which have crept in among the believers. In many cases, they look like the true wheat. During the great awakenings, there were cults such as Mormonism, and Jehovah's witnesses that rose up. During revivals throughout history, there were also many cults founded, and many within the revivals themselves were also weeds. Another example would be some anabaptists during the Protestant reformation. Some were non-Trinitarian heretics. This sort of thing will continue until the Last Day, when the World is completely sown, and the Kingdom has merged with the world. Then out of the Kingdom, the wheat and weeds are taken up, and the wheat enjoys the new creation forever, while the weeds are thrown into the Lake of Fire.

The subject of the Kingdom is often related the the study of the end times. I personally hold to amillenialism, but this study is not primarily about the end times. That being said, anyone's eschatology does influence their view of a plethora of subjects, including the view of the Kingdom. So amillenialism influences my view of the Kingdom, but I am not seeking to promote my end times view. I am trying to accurately convey what I think scripture teaches about the Kingdom itself.

Chapter 19

....

THE PARABLE OF THE MUSTARD SEED

Matt. 13:31 He put another parable before them, saying, "The kingdom of heaven is like a grain of mustard seed that a man took and sowed in his field. 32 It is the smallest of all seeds, but when it has grown it is larger than all the garden plants and becomes a tree, so that the birds of the air come and make nests in its branches."

We see here both a promise and an explanation of the growth of Christs reign. It doesn't say "your faith is like a grain of mustard seed", or "your growing in Christ through sanctification is like a grain of mustard seed" but rather, this is about Gods reign on earth in Christ starting out small, but becoming the largest as it grows. Now there are places where he does use this imagery in talking about our faith. But he can use the same picture in different ways. In Nebuchadnezzar's dream, in the book of Daniel, a stone not cut out by human hands broke the image, which represents human kingdoms, and then the stone became a mountain encompassing the world. This picture is very similar to the parable. In both, the Kingdom starts a small kingdom, yet coming with power, and it keeps growing. Jesus came as a traveling teacher and miracle worker in one of the smallest countries on earth. Most of his own people rejected him as God and messiah. He died the most brutal death in history after committing no crimes. He was buried, and on the third day, he rose from the dead. He had 120 receive the Spirit, and from there his church and his reign in the world has been growing. And it will continue to grow. Especially in the beginning stages, it's hard to believe that something so small can become so large. He oftentimes uses small, humbled, and despised things to put to shame things that seem large, pompous, and glorious. God showcases his magnificence and power by operating this way. Jesus was despised in his lifetime by those who seemed to be somebody. He continually humbled himself, to the point of death on a cross, and now he is seated higher than anyone else. He intentionally chose to have things happen the way that they did so that we would give him all the credit for doing it. Even if we are persecuted, or even if things are looking bad for the church, don't lose sight of this truth. As the Kingdom grows, there will be pruning within the Kingdom. A plant is cut back so that what grows will grow with more fruit. Cutting things off causes the right things to reproduce, and in that process we will need the faith to see that the Kingdom of Christ will not stop growing. The mustard tree will be larger than all the other plants in the garden. As it is, a once minority sect of Judaism is the world's largest religion. There are still many people who have not heard the good news of the Kingdom, so I believe the Kingdom has more growing to do yet still. Jesus mentions the birds of the air making a nest in the tree. Him saying this signifies that many people groups will pledge allegiance to the Jewish King. The gentiles being added to the Kingdom has been mentioned a lot in this book. I stress the importance of this point because it is a major theme in the New Testament. The idea that non Jews would be on equal standing before God was shocking, and even a ludicrous idea to many Jews who were Jesus's contemporaries. Statistically speaking, I know most of you reading this will be gentiles. You are not a second class citizen in God's sight. There is profit in being Jewish, because culturally there is a context for understanding what the church believes. This doesn't make Jews better Christians than Gentiles, it just means that depth of understanding might be more if you are Jewish. If you are a Gentile, you also shouldn't think you are better than Jewish people. Through them, your King came. His Kingdom does not have first and second class, only children that he loves with an everlasting love.

Chapter 20

THE PARABLE OF
THE LEAVEN

Matt. 13:33, "He told them another parable. "The kingdom of heaven is like leaven that a woman took and hid in three measures of flour, till it was all leavened."

This conveys a similar message as the parable of the mustard seed. The Kingdom is imbedded into the world via the Holy Spirit in the midst of the Church. And as disciples walk in the Spirit of God, and evangelize the nations, even in an ordinary life the Kingdom is reproducing, until the World becomes all leavened. This teaching contradicts much of the early monastic movement. This movement started early in church history, where many Christians saw corruption when Christianity became the official Roman religion, so they went into the desert to start their own communities, cut off from the outside world. They fled because they thought that the church would fall into decadence, which it did. It fell in part to the salt of the world running away to make an isolated mound of salt, making it lose its flavor. I know that in many cases, the desert fathers had some interaction with the outside world, but we are not called to be leaven separate from the dough. Something similar happened during the Jesus movement.

A bunch of people were getting saved, but due to things like the late great planet earth, and some of their end times views, much of the church at that time removed themselves from many spheres of public life. I've heard stories of some couples not having children, because they thought the rapture would happen at any moment. By and large the church then also didn't start businesses, speak into the political realm, or make an attempt to change its surrounding culture in general. Pastor Chuck Smith was a man used mightily by God, but on two occasions that I know of he said that the rapture would happen at such and such a year. An emphasis on abandoning the world as opposed to changing it by the spirit has an effect on how believers conduct themselves here and now. Those people also started Christian communes and wanted to live separate from others. It is true that the movement had a very good emphasis of evangelism, but evangelizing from a commune afar isn't allowing yourself to be the yeast of the world. I know that in the early church and at different times in church history Christians would all live together sometimes and mostly just associate with themselves, but this was out of persecution and necessity, not out of trying to put their light under a basket. The people in Jesus Movement thought the rapture would take place at any time, so there's no reason to sow into society and care about what happens in the world anyways. This gave rise to more wicked people coming into power, and trying to run the world their way, without much pushback from the church. I am apart of Calvary Chapel. I love being part of this movement. And there were many good things out of both the monastic movement and the Jesus movement. The emphasis on personal contemplation and thoughtful prayer for the monastics, and the evangelical fervor of the Jesus Movement were amazing qualities. However, both strayed when they removed themselves from the world, because it gave rise to bad things that may have been avoided. The kingdom is leaven that is in society, and in taking part in the world around you, the Kingdom's influence leavens the whole lump. This doesn't mean that if we do live as leaven that society will suddenly become perfect, or that wicked people won't ever come to power, or that everything will go the way the Christians want them to, as some tend to think. It does mean that the Kingdom is leavened into the world and that it does bring about change. It's true that we are not to be of the world, and we are called to be separate in that we are radically different than those around us. We are supposed to live differently. But we are called to be in the world. Through the church in the world, the Kingdom spreads, and changes the nature of the dough. If the light of the world removes itself from the world, subsequently darkness will then take over. This becomes a self-fulfilling prophecy. We say "everything is gonna get darker and darker towards the end" so we remove ourselves from the darkness that is there. Then it gets darker in the world. Rinse and repeat. So this parable has much relevance to us today. It shows us how God intends to have his Kingdom grow in the world.

Chapter 21

THE PARABLES OF THE TREASURE IN THE FIELD, AND THE PEARL OF GREAT VALUE

Matt. 13:44 "The kingdom of heaven is like treasure hidden in a field, which a man found and covered up. Then in his joy he goes and sells all that he has and buys that field.

Matt. 13:45 "Again, the kingdom of heaven is like a merchant in search of fine pearls, 46 who, on finding one pearl of great value, went and sold all that he had and bought it."

When reading this, I used to think that the church is the man or the merchant in these parables. That we in our joy give up everything to follow Jesus. While there is some truth to that idea, I don't think contextually this is what Jesus was primarily saying. In a previous parable, the man is mentioned sowing seeds. In his own words, Jesus is saying that he is the man. Likewise, in these two parables, I believe that the man or merchant is Christ. It is written elsewhere "who for the joy that was set before him endured the cross, despising the shame, and is seated at the right hand of the throne of God"

This statement in Hebrews 12:2 sheds light on the two parables. Christ in his joy gave up everything for us, that he may purchase us by his blood. We are the pearl, and the treasure. And at the same time, Christ is given the Kingdom. Jesus said, "For the Father judges no one, but has given all judgment to the Son, 23 that all may honor the Son, just as they honor the Father. " John 5:22-23.

We see that the church and the Kingdom are also closely related. The question we have to ask is this: is the church and Kingdom the same thing? Are these synonymous terms? Yes and no.

Revelation 1:5-6"To him who loves us and has freed us from our sins by his blood 6 and made us a kingdom, priests to his God and Father, to him be glory and dominion forever and ever. Amen."

So in a sense, the church is the Kingdom. Christ has made us as the Kingdom. The church makes up the temple of God, and the Kingdom of God. We receive the Kingdom, possess the Kingdom, and inherit it. But in a sense, no, the church is not the kingdom of God. We are given the Kingdom, and it operates through us. God delegates his authority through his church. The parable of the Minas sheds light on this.

Luke 9:11-27 "As they heard these things, he proceeded to tell a parable, because he was near to Jerusalem, and because they supposed that the kingdom of God was to appear immediately. 12 He said therefore, "A nobleman went into a far country to receive for himself a kingdom and then return. 13 Calling ten of his servants, he gave them ten minas, and said to them, 'Engage in business until I come.' 14 But his citizens hated him and sent a delegation after him, saying, 'We do not want this man to reign over us.' 15 When he returned, having received the kingdom, he ordered these servants to whom he had given the money to be called to him, that he might know what they had gained by doing business. 16 The first came before him, saying, 'Lord, your mina has made ten minas more.' 17 And he said to him, 'Well done, good servant! Because you have been faithful in a very little, you shall have authority over ten cities.' 18 And the second came, saying, 'Lord, your mina has made five minas.' 19 And he said to him, 'And you are to be over five cities.' 20 Then another came, saying, 'Lord, here is your mina, which I kept laid away in a handkerchief; 21 for I was afraid of you, because you are a severe man. You take what you did not deposit, and reap what you did not sow.' 22 He said to him, 'I will condemn you with your own words, you wicked servant! You knew that I was a severe man, taking what I did not deposit and reaping what I did not sow? 23 Why then did you not put my money in the bank, and at my coming I might have collected it with interest?' 24 And he said to those who stood by, 'Take the mina from him, and give it to the one who has the ten minas.' 25 And they said to him, 'Lord, he has ten minas!' 26 'I tell you that to everyone who has, more will be given, but from the one who has not, even what he has will be taken away. 27 But as for these enemies of mine, who did not want me to reign over them, bring them here and slaughter them before me.'"

In this life, the servants of Jesus are to engage in Kingdom business. By our faithfulness in stewardship, we do just that. We extended the rule of God by using what he gave us for his glory. And at the end, when he returns with the Kingdom coming fully, those who were faithful with what they had received will be given more authority in the new creation. So we are as the Kingdom, serving and ruling in it. But we are not as the church, the Kingdom itself. We see that the Kingdom grows through our obedience and faithfulness to Christ. We have also seen that Christ gives us of his authority now, and in more fullness in the age to come.

Chapter 22

....

PARABLE OF THE FISH
IN THE NETS

Matt. 13:47 "Again, the kingdom of heaven is like a net that was thrown into the sea and gathered fish of every kind. 48 When it was full, men drew it ashore and sat down and sorted the good into containers but threw away the bad. 49 So it will be at the end of the age. The angels will come out and separate the evil from the righteous 50 and throw them into the fiery furnace. In that place there will be weeping and gnashing of teeth."

The King is coming. Mark 14:62 " And Jesus said, "I am, and you will see the Son of Man seated at the right hand of Power, and coming with the clouds of heaven."

This parable teaches us that he will return, with his reward, and recompense. The Kingdom will come in fullness then, when the new heaven and earth are created. The wicked will be cast out, with bodies prepared for destruction, and the righteous will receive their glorified bodies. This is known as the general resurrection of the dead. At the time of the second coming of Jesus, all people who have died before his return will be resurrected for judgment, receiving good and bad things, depending on their works. Daniel 12:2, "And many of those who sleep in the dust of the earth shall awake, some to everlasting life, and some to shame and everlasting contempt." Daniel prophesied that the dead will be raised up on the Day of Judgment. This means that Jesus will judge the whole person, not just their souls. He told us that God has the capability to destroy both body and soul in Hell. If there is no body when they are judged, then there is no way to destroy it in Hell. Those who are not dead when he returns will be changed if they are Christians. They will put on the new body at that time. The people who are alive then will also be judged. The Bible describes people crying and hoping to be crushed because of their fear of God's wrath coming upon them. The people of God are the good fish, and the bad fish represent everyone else in the World. If the Kingdom is like a net, it means that the Kingdom is in and around the world now. If not, how could the angels take up and sort out the people? This was the question being asked in chapter 4. Where is Heaven? Jesus said it is in our midst. The Day of Judgement is rightly thought of as the most terrifying day in history. Paradoxically, for Christians this is the ultimate day of salvation. We will be judged, but not like the World is judged, because we are in the Book of Life. The place prepared for us will finally arrive, and we will see our God face to face. Colossians 3:4, "When Christ who is your life appears, then you also will appear with him in glory." Heaven was cast like a net on earth, and will take up all on the last day.

Chapter 23
....

TRAINED KINGDOM SCRIBES

Matt. 13:51 "Have you understood all these things?" They said to him, "Yes." 52 And he said to them, "Therefore every scribe who has been trained for the kingdom of heaven is like a master of a house, who brings out of his treasure what is new and what is old."

This seems like a strange way to end the parables he spoke in Matthew 13. Here is how I would interpret this: Jesus asks if they understand what the taught in the parables. The disciples said they did. With that, Jesus is teaching that every scribe, or someone who we would probably call a scholar today, and if not a scholar, then someone who studies and understands the scriptures, based on the understanding that the Holy Spirit gives them, brings truth out of both old and new covenants. If they are being trained for the Kingdom, it seems that the treasure that is brought out is revelations of the prophesied king, and how his Kingdom functions. Also, it seems like Jesus is here talking about the parables themselves. He asks if they get the parables, then proceeds to say because of that, scribes trained in the Kingdom bring out treasure. The treasure is the understanding of the parables Jesus spoke, and the teaching of those parables to others. We as learners of Jesus are to be Kingdom scribes, meaning, we are to look at the scriptures with an eye to see and learn more about the Kingdom. This is not a secondary theme to Jesus, but the Kingdom is a central theme in his teachings and ministry. This isn't only for brainiacs and academics, but for the whole church. We are to be a church of scholarly people. Just like the Berean church in the book of Acts, who inquired from the scriptures to see if what the Apostle Paul said was the truth. Some believers in the body of Christ have a teaching gift, and some have more wisdom than others. Everyone does not understand everything equally. Everyone should still sit at the feet of Jesus, and remain in his word. A small select group of Christian's who think they are the only ones who can understand scripture are wrong. We are all anointed with the Holy Spirit. The anointing will teach us all things. We have to test teachings by scripture, because we are fallible, but there is also not an elite class of theologians who alone understand scripture. Being a kingdom scribe is the duty of the whole church.

Chapter 24

....

PARABLE OF THE UNFORGIVING SERVANT

Matthew 18: 23-35 "Therefore the kingdom of heaven may be compared to a king who wished to settle accounts with his servants. 24 When he began to settle, one was brought to him who owed him ten thousand talents. 25 And since he could not pay, his master ordered him to be sold, with his wife and children and all that he had, and payment to be made. 26 So the servant fell on his knees, imploring him, 'Have patience with me, and I will pay you everything.' 27 And out of pity for him, the master of that servant released him and forgave him the debt. 28 But when that same servant went out, he found one of his fellow servants who owed him a hundred denarii, and seizing him, he began to choke him, saying, 'Pay what you owe.' 29 So his fellow servant fell down and pleaded with him, 'Have patience with me, and I will pay you.' 30 He refused and went and put him in prison until he should pay the debt. 31 When his fellow servants saw what had taken place, they were greatly distressed, and they went and reported to their master all that had taken place. 32 Then his master summoned him and said to him, 'You wicked servant! I forgave you all that debt because you pleaded with me. 33 And should not you have had mercy on your fellow servant, as I had mercy on you?' 34 And in anger his master delivered him to the jailers, until he should pay all his debt. 35 So also my heavenly Father will do to every one of you, if you do not forgive your brother from your heart."

One of the highest values in Heaven is mercy. In this parable, God the Father is the master. When the servant sees that everything is taken from him due to his debt, including his life, he begs for mercy, and vows restitution. He is given mercy, and restitution is not required. God forgave his debt. Then, the servant finds a fellow servant. He demands his money, and does not give mercy. Then he was thrown in jail. The Father forgives us first. He is merciful to us. And when that happens, we are also to be merciful to everyone, especially fellow servants of the Kingdom. Our God and Father delights in mercy, so much so that he wants his citizens to be like he is in showing mercy. He is so serious about this that he says that if we refuse to do so, we have no place in his Kingdom. Jesus said "blessed are the merciful, for they shall receive mercy" in Matthew 5:7 not "blessed are the unmerciful". In the our Father prayer, the only thing that we do is forgive our debtors. One of the most practical ways to walk in the Kingdom is to forgive and show mercy when others do us wrong. In reality, God always forgives us much more than we will ever forgive others. We owe him exponentially more than others owe us. In the parable, ten thousand talents was what was owed to God. In today's money, this would be $3,480,000,000. That is 3.48 billion. What did the one servant owe to the other? In today's money, 100 denarius would be roughly $17,000. Let us as adopted princes and princesses of God the father walk in his Kingdom in a worthy manner, by forgiving debt, and delighting in mercy. Jesus said "go and learn what this means: I desire mercy and not sacrifice" Matthew 9:13.

Chapter 25

. . . .

PARABLE OF THE LABORERS IN THE VINEYARD

Matthew 20:1-16"For the kingdom of heaven is like a master of a house who went out early in the morning to hire laborers for his vineyard. 2 After agreeing with the laborers for a denarius a day, he sent them into his vineyard. 3 And going out about the third hour he saw others standing idle in the marketplace, 4 and to them he said, 'You go into the vineyard too, and whatever is right I will give you.' 5 So they went. Going out again about the sixth hour and the ninth hour, he did the same. 6 And about the eleventh hour he went out and found others standing. And he said to them, 'Why do you stand here idle all day?' 7 They said to him, 'Because no one has hired us.' He said to them, 'You go into the vineyard too.' 8 And when evening came, the owner of the vineyard said to his foreman, 'Call the laborers and pay them their wages, beginning with the last, up to the first.' 9 And when those hired about the eleventh hour came, each of them received a denarius. 10 Now when those hired first came, they thought they would receive more, but each of them also received a denarius. 11 And on receiving it they grumbled at the master of the house, 12 saying, 'These last worked only one hour, and you have made them equal to us who have borne the burden of the day and the scorching heat.' 13 But he replied to one of them, 'Friend, I am doing you no wrong. Did you not agree with me for a denarius? 14 Take what belongs to you and go. I choose to give to this last worker as I give to you. 15 Am I not allowed to do what I choose with what belongs to me? Or do you begrudge my generosity?' 16 So the last will be first, and the first last."

The principle we have here is another important value, because the phrase "So the last will be first, and the first last." is repeated four times by Jesus in his teachings. This is the point of the parable. We see here themes of humility and entitlement, and the grace of God. The agreement that the first labors had was the same as the last. Whether you submit to the lordship of Christ at the beginning of your life, or the end, you receive eternal life, and will rule with him. Some seem to think this is unfair. They think that because they've been in the Kingdom longer, they deserve more than those who wasted their lives then repented at the end. What they fail to realize is that they don't deserve the offer either. We don't deserve our opportunity to be in Christ, him offering us salvation and an inheritance is pure grace. Some of us who have been Christians since childhood fall into the trap of thinking that doing his will longer makes us worthy to receive more than what Jesus offered us.

"And on receiving it they grumbled at the master of the house, 12 saying, 'These last worked only one hour, and you have made them equal to us who have borne the burden of the day and the scorching heat.' 13 But he replied to one of them, 'Friend, I am doing you no wrong. Did you not agree with me for a denarius? 14 Take what belongs to you and go. I choose to give to this last worker as I give to you. 15 Am I not allowed to do what I choose with what belongs to me? Or do you begrudge my generosity?" God is fully within his right to give whatever he wants, to whoever he wants. God will never owe us anything.

Notice Jesus in this parable didn't say that he owed any of the labors anything. The wage here doesn't mean that. The wage being paid is him giving us our promised inheritance, based on us trusting in his promise to give it. We should walk in humility, and that humility looks like us not complaining because we "borne the burden of the day and the scorching heat", and in a general sense we get the same thing as those who didn't suffer for believing his promise. When the apostles were beaten in the book of Acts, they rejoiced because they were counted worthy to suffer for the name of Jesus. We aren't even worthy enough to suffer for God. Let us not be entitled, but instead rejoice in the character of God, who always keeps his word. Jesus said "fear not, little flock, for it is your fathers good pleasure to give you the kingdom" Luke 12:32

Chapter 26
. . . .

THE PARABLE OF THE
BAD TENANTS AND THE
WEDDING FEAST

Matthew 21:33–22:14 "Hear another parable. There was a master
of a house who planted a vineyard and put a fence around it and
dug a winepress in it and built a tower and leased it to tenants,
and went into another country. 34 When the season for fruit drew
near, he sent his servants to the tenants to get his fruit. 35 And the
tenants took his servants and beat one, killed another, and stoned
another. 36 Again he sent other servants, more than the first. And
they did the same to them. 37 Finally he sent his son to them,
saying, 'They will respect my son.' 38 But when the tenants saw
the son, they said to themselves, 'This is the heir. Come, let us kill
him and have his inheritance.' 39 And they took him and threw
him out of the vineyard and killed him. 40 When therefore the
owner of the vineyard comes, what will he do to those tenants?"
41 They said to him, "He will put those wretches to a miserable
death and let out the vineyard to other tenants who will give him
the fruits in their seasons."

Matt. 21:42 Jesus said to them, "Have you never read in the
Scriptures:"'The stone that the builders rejected has become the

cornerstone; this was the Lord's doing, and it is marvelous in our eyes'? Matt. 21:43 Therefore I tell you, the kingdom of God will be taken away from you and given to a people producing its fruits. 44 And the one who falls on this stone will be broken to pieces; and when it falls on anyone, it will crush him."

Matt. 21:45 When the chief priests and the Pharisees heard his parables, they perceived that he was speaking about them. 46 And although they were seeking to arrest him, they feared the crowds, because they held him to be a prophet.

Matt. 22:1 And again Jesus spoke to them in parables, saying, 2 "The kingdom of heaven may be compared to a king who gave a wedding feast for his son, 3 and sent his servants to call those who were invited to the wedding feast, but they would not come. 4 Again he sent other servants, saying, 'Tell those who are invited, "See, I have prepared my dinner, my oxen and my fat calves have been slaughtered, and everything is ready. Come to the wedding feast."' 5 But they paid no attention and went off, one to his farm, another to his business, 6 while the rest seized his servants, treated them shamefully, and killed them. 7 The king was angry, and he sent his troops and destroyed those murderers and burned their city. 8 Then he said to his servants, 'The wedding feast is ready, but those invited were not worthy. 9 Go therefore to the main roads and invite to the wedding feast as many as you find.' 10 And those servants went out into the roads and gathered all whom they found, both bad and good. So the wedding hall was filled with guests.

Matt. 22:11 "But when the king came in to look at the guests, he saw there a man who had no wedding garment. 12 And he said to him, 'Friend, how did you get in here without a wedding garment?' And he was speechless. 13 Then the king said to the attendants, 'Bind him hand and foot and cast him into the outer darkness. In that place there will be weeping and gnashing of teeth.' 14 For many are called, but few are chosen."

Just to give some context to this portion of scripture, in the previous verses Jesus was rebuking the Pharisees, and telling them that Israel is being cut off by and large for their rejection of him as their messiah. Since they reject the King, the Kingdom is stripped from them. The Pharisees were blinded by their interpretation of what the Christ would come to accomplish, and they wanted to hold on to their positions of authority over the people. Jesus begins by giving a synopsis of Israel's history when the word of the Lord came to them through prophets. The language of the vineyard as Israel would not have been foreign to his hearers, as Jesus here is expounding upon Isaiah 5:1-7 which says,

"Let me sing for my beloved my love song concerning his vineyard: My beloved had a vineyard on a very fertile hill.2 He dug it and cleared it of stones,and planted it with choice vines; he built a watchtower in the midst of it, and hewed out a wine vat in it; and he looked for it to yield grapes, but it yielded wild grapes. Is. 5:3 And now, O inhabitants of Jerusalem and men of Judah, judge between me and my vineyard.4 What more was there to do for my vineyard, that I have not done in it? When I looked for it to yield grapes, why did it yield wild grapes? Is. 5:5 And now I will tell you what I will do to my vineyard. I will remove its hedge, and it shall be devoured; I will break down its wall, and it shall be trampled down.6 I will make it a waste; it shall not be pruned or hoed, and briers and thorns shall grow up; I will also command the clouds that they rain no rain upon it. Is. 5:7 For the vineyard of the LORD of hosts is the house of Israel, and the men of Judah are his pleasant planting; and he looked for justice, but behold, bloodshed; for righteousness, but behold, an outcry!"

Israel did not bear fruit to God, walking in faith or remaining loyal to him, even after him cultivating them and blessing them as a nation. But the Father in his mercy sent many prophets to them over the course of centuries. They persecuted them to varying degrees. The culmination of this was the Father sending the Son to Israel, so that they would repent and come back to the Lord. Instead of doing so, they threw him out of the vineyard, which points to Jesus dying outside of Jerusalem. Then Jesus asks what will happen after this event. And the Pharisees answer correctly "They said to him, "He will put those wretches to a miserable death and let out the vineyard to other tenants who will give him the fruits in their seasons." Jesus then quotes psalm 118 about the rejected cornerstone, which is referring to himself. He is the one who was rejected but became King. The Kingdom was taken away from Israel, and came to the gentiles, who will bear fruit to God until the fullness of the gentiles is completed. When Jesus was before the high priest he says, "And Jesus said, "I am, and you will see the Son of Man seated at the right hand of Power, and coming with the clouds of heaven."- Mark 14:62. And also, Matthew 6:28 "Truly, I say to you, there are some standing here who will not taste death until they see the Son of Man coming in his Kingdom"

I don't think he was only speaking about the second coming, because he was eluding to this passage in Daniel:

Daniel 7:13-15 " "I saw in the night visions, and behold, with the clouds of heaven there came one like a son of man, and he came to the Ancient of Days and was presented before him.14
And to him was given dominion and glory and a kingdom, that all peoples, nations, and languages should serve him; his dominion is an everlasting dominion, which shall not pass away, and his kingdom one that shall not be destroyed."

I do think that the passage in Mark, where Jesus was standing before the high priest, he was eluding to his second coming. The son of man in Daniel was a divine figure, because only God rides on the clouds of heaven in the Old Testament. Also, John when talking about the appearing of Christ said he would be riding on the clouds. So this isn't completely about Jesus receiving the Kingdom, but we read that the coming on the clouds was Jesus coming to the Father to receive the Kingdom, and that gentiles would be included in it. Jesus in Matthew was telling the Pharisees about this. This is why they wanted to arrest him. Jesus told them that whoever falls on the stone, they will be broken. When we submit to his lordship, we die to ourselves. But whoever it falls on, they will be ground to powder. In 70 AD, Jerusalem was utterly destroyed, and anyone who doesn't submit to the lordship of Christ, they will be utterly destroyed. The Kingdom of the anointed one being stripped away from Israel and going to the gentiles is what the second parable in the Matthew passage is about. The Jews rejected coming to the wedding feast, which is a picture of Jesus's Kingdom, and so "The king was angry, and he sent his troops and destroyed those murderers and burned their city", which is Jerusalem. And since they refused to acknowledge the salvation that God offered them, the good news came to the gentiles, who gladly came to the feast. This was done to make the Jews jealous, and in doing so they would come back and accept their messiah.

Jesus taught us so much about the Kingdom within the parables. He taught a lot about how the Kingdom functions, and what the Kingdom does. This study is far from complete. I would encourage you to read the parables for yourself, and ask, "What does this tell me about the Kingdom?" He gives wisdom liberally and without partiality.

THE GOOD NEWS OF
THE KINGDOM

In the first century, Jesus and the people of God proclaimed the gospel of the Kingdom along with the message of repentance. We do preach repentance today, but many times in evangelism do not preach his kingship, or the coming Kingdom. We must reclaim this idea when sharing our faith with others, because of it's relevancy in God's redemptive history and plan.

Chapter 27

....

THE KINGDOM THE SIGNS PROCLAIM

During the public ministry of Jesus, as well as the apostles, the Good News of the Kingdom was a central theme. So much so, that Jesus says in Luke 4:43 "I must preach the good news of the kingdom of God to the other towns as well; for I was sent for this purpose."

Sometimes we like to compartmentalize the things they did as they went out. Sometimes they preached, sometimes they healed the sick, sometimes they discipled people. However, the scriptures teach that these different actions were all embedded in proclaiming the Kingdom.

Matthew 9:35 "And Jesus went throughout all the cities and villages, teaching in their synagogues and proclaiming the gospel of the kingdom and healing every disease and every affliction."

Matthew 10:7-8 "And proclaim as you go, saying, 'The kingdom of heaven is at hand.' 8 Heal the sick, raise the dead, cleanse lepers, cast out demons. You received without paying; give without pay."

But that was just for Christ and his apostles you might say. The modern argument is that the different signs or healings or deliverance were only to confirm the message preached. While it is true that the apostles did the "signs of an apostle" and that this did confirm the message, both the signs and the message working together are more nuanced than just that. Jesus said,

Matthew 12:28 "But if it is by the Spirit of God that I cast out demons, then the kingdom of God has come upon you."

We learn from this passage that when Jesus casted out demons, the Kingdom came upon them. The deliverance was a proclamation of authority. The message of the Kingdom here is that Jesus, the son of God, is King over evil spirits. Healing showcases this also.

Luke 9:11 "When the crowds learned it, they followed him, and he welcomed them and spoke to them of the kingdom of God and cured those who had need of healing."

We learn too that the Kingdom is a place of freedom, the Son of Man came to set the captives free.

Luke 4:17-21 "And the scroll of the prophet Isaiah was given to him. He unrolled the scroll and found the place where it was written, 18 "The Spirit of the Lord is upon me, because he has anointed me to proclaim good news to the poor. He has sent me to proclaim liberty to the captives and recovering of sight to the blind, to set at liberty those who are oppressed, 19   to proclaim the year of the Lord's favor."

20 And he rolled up the scroll and gave it back to the attendant and sat down. And the eyes of all in the synagogue were fixed on him. 21 And he began to say to them, "Today this Scripture has been fulfilled in your hearing."

All Christians would agree that Jesus is Lord. We believe that he is the "Christ". We get this from the Greek word "Christos" and the Hebrew word "mashiach". Both of these mean "anointed one" kings in the Old Testament were anointed king. The anointed one is a kingly title. So every time Jesus preached, taught, or did signs, it was a demonstration of his lordship, and of the Father's Kingdom. It was the Father's stamp of approval, proving that the Father sent the Son, and the Kingdom would be given to the Son. The Son, having authority on earth, dispensed his authority to his disciples,

Luke 10:9 "Heal the sick in it and say to them, 'The kingdom of God has come near to you.'

The apostles were commissioned to spread the Kingdom. That didn't happen by word only, but by the message and the accompanying signs. But what about the church? You might ask. That was only for apostles. But that's not true of the first century church.

Acts 8:5-8 "Philip went down to the city of Samaria and proclaimed to them the Christ. 6 And the crowds with one accord paid attention to what was being said by Philip, when they heard him and saw the signs that he did. 7 For unclean spirits, crying out with a loud voice, came out of many who had them, and many who were paralyzed or lame were healed. 8 So there was much joy in that city."

Philip the evangelist was at least one exception. He is called "the evangelist" but his evangelical career had signs and wonders, healings and exorcisms, as well as a call for people to repent. If someone wants to say that this is just an exception to the rule, then Barnabas was another exception.

Acts 15:12 "And all the assembly fell silent, and they listened to Barnabas and Paul as they related what signs and wonders God had done through them among the Gentiles."

To belabor the point, the Galatian church had the gifts. The Roman church, Corinthian church, and the people who Peter wrote to all had different gifts, some supernatural, to build up the church and to proclaim what Gods Kingdom is, and how to live in light of it. Otherwise why would Paul and Peter teach about the gifts? Why would there be chapters dedicated to teaching about how to operate in the gifts properly, and encouraging them to seek these things if the church didn't have the gifts? The same question can be asked if the gifts of the Spirit aren't for today. So we see that the church had been given these things as a proclamation of the Kingdom. To bring balance, it is true that an adulterous generation always looks for a sign. Many people wanted to see Jesus's miracles, but never accept him as their master. People then and now want the benefits of the Kingdom, without having to pledge allegiance to the King. This is blasphemous and disgusting. We want to be glorified and reign with Christ, but we want nothing to do with suffering with him, and for him. If we spend all of our time chasing miracles, and don't desire glorifying Jesus in our character, we are just seeking signs, and thus reveal where our loyalty truly lies. We see this struggle even in the disciples. The mother of James and John came to Jesus, asking that they may sit on his right and left hand in his glory. The disciples frequently argued as to who was the greatest. But at the night of Jesus's betrayal, they all fell away. It was only at the giving of the Holy Spirit, and them being born again that this persuasion died. After the Spirt, the apostles praised God and rejoiced for being counted worthy to suffer for the sake of Christ. They still would reign with Christ. And they still had miracles done through them. So the solution for the problem of disloyalty to Christ isn't throwing the gifts and promises out the window. The solution is to let the Holy Spirit do his work, bringing us into the submission of Christ. Then, for us to proclaim the Gospel of the Kingdom, in the power of the Holy Spirit. And if exorcisms and healings happen, it is to witness about the Kingdom, and something we should praise God for.

Chapter 28

....

RELEVANCE AND RENEWAL

The message is not out of date. The Kingdom is still a central reality that the church must preach. Jesus didn't only speak about the Kingdom during his earthly ministry, but even after his resurrection.

Acts 1:3 "He presented himself alive to them after his suffering by many proofs, appearing to them during forty days and speaking about the kingdom of God."

When Jesus ascended to the right hand of the Father, the Holy Spirit was poured out upon the church. And the church also had the kingdom as a central theme.

Acts 8:12 "But when they believed Philip as he preached good news about the kingdom of God and the name of Jesus Christ, they were baptized, both men and women."

Acts 19:8 "And he entered the synagogue and for three months spoke boldly, reasoning and persuading them about the kingdom of God."

Acts 28:23 "When they had appointed a day for him, they came to him at his lodging in greater numbers. From morning till evening he expounded to them, testifying to the kingdom of God and trying to convince them about Jesus both from the Law of Moses and from the Prophets."

The book of Acts ends with Paul preaching the Kingdom.

Acts 28:30-31 "He lived there two whole years at his own expense, and welcomed all who came to him, 31 proclaiming the kingdom of God and teaching about the Lord Jesus Christ with all boldness and without hindrance."

John the Baptist, Jesus, the apostles, and the first century church all were heralds of the Kingdom. So let us as Jesus's body not set aside this truth, and start walking in his footsteps. We are to be transformed from the worldly way of thinking, and in knowledge be renewed in the image of our creator. The Gospel is not about "praying this prayer to go to heaven when you die" nor is it just an entrance into a world religion. The good news is that God himself has entered the human race, becoming a man, born of a virgin, and lived up to Gods law and standard perfectly, to restore us who haven't kept the standard either by our nature or our deeds, was crucified for our sins, and in that crucifixion he conquered also the principalities, powers, and swallowed up death in victory. He was buried, and on the third day he rose again, justifying his people, and being the firstborn from the dead, that in everything he is Lord. He ascended to the right hand of the Father, and received the Kingdom. We walk in his Kingdom now, and will inherit it later. All of his enemies will be put under his feet, and he will come again, bringing the Kingdom in fullness. He will give his people resurrected bodies, and we will reign forever with him in the new heavens and earth. All of this was promised beforehand by God through his prophets. We as his people are to be witnesses and signs of God's saving power, and model in ourselves by holiness and sanctification what heaven on earth looks like. We are to set our minds on heaven above, where Christ is, and to put the death what is earthly in us, that is, the things that are contrary to being a citizen in heaven.

1 Corinthians 6:9-11 "Or do you not know that the unrighteous will not inherit the kingdom of God? Do not be deceived: neither the sexually immoral, nor idolaters, nor adulterers, nor men who practice homosexuality, 10 nor thieves, nor the greedy, nor drunkards, nor revilers, nor swindlers will inherit the kingdom of God. 11 And such were some of you. But you were washed, you were sanctified, you were justified in the name of the Lord Jesus Christ and by the Spirit of our God.

The transformation is only attainable through the Holy Spirit, who was given to us when we are born again from above. He is like a down payment for our inheritance into new life, until we possess the promised Kingdom.

Chapter 29

....

CONCLUSION MOVING FORWARD

This was written because I myself do not understand the Kingdom completely. I have heard that if you start expressing something you don't understand, you begin to understand it. This book was born out of my ignorance of the subject, and a hunger to better grasp it. This also was not written to be the most exhaustive study of this subject, but rather it was written to spread awareness about something I haven't heard a lot about from the church. This is not a final word on the Kingdom, but is meant to start conversations, and further inquiry about it.

My admonition to the church is to not keep on deemphasizing the importance of the Kingdom because we don't know what to make of it. Rather, we should recognize that the Gospel message is intertwined with the Kingdom. And let us now live our lives in a way that says "your Kingdom come, your will be done on earth as it is in heaven". All authority on heaven and on earth has been given to Christ, therefore let us go with that authority and work to extend his reign. We know that anything done for his sake will never be in vain.

I say to the church, be encouraged by Daniel 7:18 "But the saints of the Most High shall receive the kingdom and possess the kingdom forever, forever and ever."

And to the world, I say "The time is fulfilled, and the kingdom of God is at hand; repent and believe in the gospel."
Mark 1:15

Printed in the United States
by Baker & Taylor Publisher Services

Printed in the United States
by Baker & Taylor Publisher Services